KU-701-728

Help Your Child with Literacy Ages 7–11

Caroline Coxon

continuum

Continuum International Publishing Group
The Tower Building, 11 York Road, London SE1 7NX
80 Maiden Lane, Suite 704, New York, NY 10038

www.continuumbooks.com

© Caroline Coxon 2009

Illustrations by Clare Jarvis

All rights reserved. No part of this publication may be reproduced or
transmitted in any form or by any means, electronic or mechanical,
including photocopying, recording, or any information storage or
retrieval system, without prior permission in writing from the publishers.

Caroline Coxon has asserted her right under the Copyright, Designs and
Patents Act, 1988, to be identified as Author of this work.

British Library Cataloguing-in-Publication Data
A catalogue record for this book is available from the British Library.

ISBN: 9781847064349 (paperback)

Library of Congress Cataloging-in-Publication Data
A catalog record for this book is available from the Library of Congress.

Designed and typeset by Kenneth Burnley, Wirral, Cheshire
Printed and bound in Great Britain by Ashford Colour Press Ltd

Contents

Introduction

Why is literacy important?

Imagine what your life would be like if you couldn't read and write. Think of all the everyday tasks that would become a struggle, and how difficult it would be to learn anything at all. That's how important literacy is!

Is this the book you're looking for?

Are you the parent or carer of a child who has been at school for two or three years? Are you keen to help with school work at home – but worried that you might not do a good job?

Or perhaps you're just starting out as a teaching assistant, or you're a person who helps older children with reading at the local primary school?

Then this is just the book for you!

Go to any high-street bookshop and you will find shelves and shelves of workbooks for children, full of promises to help improve their literacy skills and do better with SATs or other school tests. Of course you want your child to do well; of course you want to help as much as possible, but with such a bewildering array of titles in front of you, sometimes it's difficult to know where to start.

With a younger child, just starting out at school, things often seem less complicated. Your child is probably keen and happy to spend time on reading and writing because they're something new. Older children can be much more difficult to motivate and would *definitely* prefer to be playing computer games or doing things with their friends, instead of brushing up on their punctuation and grammar!

The thing to remember is that it doesn't have to be dull; it doesn't have to be a struggle; it can be the most wonderful time you spend with your child. What better way to pass half an hour than to have fun learning together and improving your child's chances to do well and be happy at school?

This book is just for you. Its aim is to show you how you can help a 7 to 11-year-old child with literacy. It is for people who use English, whether or not it is their first language. It explains all the jargon and gives you lots of ideas for activities that are fun, as well as useful. Most of all, it will give you the confidence you need to help your child. It won't take you long to realize that you are exactly the right person for the job!

About this book

He or she?

It goes without saying that your child is either a girl or a boy! Rather than say 'he or she' each time, which is very tedious, sometimes 'he' is used and sometimes 'she' is used in this book.

Key to the symbols

 This indicates a **good idea**. These are mostly activities that will add variety to the time you spend helping your child.

 This indicates things to **watch out** for! Lots of children have exactly the same problems. With these tips, you can be one step ahead!

 When a technical term is used, you might think **'What's this?'** Words are explained immediately, so you don't have to spend time turning to the Glossary on page 75, where all the terms are listed.

How to start

The plan

This is something for both of you, not a punishment for your child for failing to get top marks at school. There are certain things that will have to be agreed upon before you start. Sort out all the ground rules together. When you will do this. What you will do. For how long.

> Why not ask your child to write out the rules when you've agreed on them? You could stick them to the wall in your chosen workplace.

Talk to your child's teacher. You're a team and you'll be able to help each other to help your child. Teachers love it when parents and carers show an interest in supporting the work that goes on in school.

The time

Decide between you when is the best time to get together. It might be before school, or may be after. It's up to the two of you to decide. You might want to stick to the same time each day, or choose on a daily basis, depending on what's happening.

Decide how long the session will be. It's much better to have a daily session of a few minutes than a lengthy one once a week. You never know, you might be having such a good time that you'll go on for longer without even realizing it!

The place

Choose somewhere distraction-free and comfortable, away from the TV and lots of background noise. If it could be the same place each time, then better still. Together, you could set it up with everything you need.

Plan a shopping trip together to buy new pencils, exercise books and anything else you think you'll need. It won't cost much and will be such a positive way to start.

The mood

It's up to you, as the adult, to create it, so if possible make sure it's when you're not tired or rushed:

- Be prepared – have everything ready and know what you're going to do, so the pace is lively at all times.

- Be relaxed – it's not meant to be an ordeal for either of you.

- Be positive – there is always, *always* something good to be found in anyone's work, as well as things that could be improved. Don't pick out every little mistake. Decide together what might need extra work. Encourage at every opportunity.

- Always end on a positive note, so next time will be something to look forward to.

- Do it yourself! How can you encourage your child to read and write if she never sees you doing it?

Most of all . . .

Have fun – always include games and fun activities. This book will help you with some ideas if you get stuck.

There are some difficulties your child might have which will affect her literacy skills, indeed, everything she does at school. These are not anything to be alarmed about, but it is important to notice and do something about it. Some problems are easily spotted when your child is much younger but others don't necessarily show up until later when school work is more demanding. Sorting things out can be simple and will make all the difference.

Being left-handed

In the 'old days' if you were left-handed, efforts were made to force you to use your right hand instead. Fortunately those days are long gone!

■ About 10 per cent of people are left-handed.

■ More boys are left-handed than girls.

In English we write from left to right. This means that a left-hander can't see what he's writing because his hand covers it and this can makes things tricky. In addition, it's awkward to hold a pen or pencil in the usual way.

Find an older child or adult who is also left-handed to teach your child how to write comfortably.

There are plenty of special pens and other equipment that are available. You could buy from the following places:

www.lefthandedchildren.org/

www.anythingleft-handed.co.uk/kids_help.html

Here are some other tips. You might even want to tell your child's teacher!

■ Be sure the desk or table your child is using is the right height.

■ Position paper so it's completely to the left of the child's midline.

■ Angle the paper so it's parallel to the child's forearm.

> You could stick tape to the desk in an outline of a sheet of paper in the correct position.

■ Make sure your left-handed child doesn't have a right-handed child sitting on his left side because they will get in each other's way!

■ Make sure the desk is clear to the left of your child so he has space to write.

■ Sit opposite your child, if you are right-handed, not next to him. That way when you write he will be able to mirror your actions.

Poor eyesight

Iain Anderson, Chairman of the Eyecare Trust, knows a lot about eyes. He tells us that one in five children have visual problems and only a third of them are receiving professional care. He adds 'Most parents assume that children will have their sight checked regularly during the school years as part of wider health monitoring, but unfortunately this is not the case.'

Poor eyesight is something that could affect learning abilities and reading development, which can, in turn, lead to a child having low self-esteem or exhibiting bad behaviour.

Eye tests are free for children and it is a good idea to have this done once a year, even if you don't think there is any need.

Colour blindness

Also known as colour vision deficiency, it's also something to be tested by an optician if your child is having problems in class, because it just might be the reason. For example, a child may not be able to see yellow writing on a green background, so she will struggle to keep up. For young children it's much harder to explain to an adult than simply 'I can't see very well'.

You could try out different colours of pens and paper at home to see if any combination is more difficult for your child to see. Then inform her teacher!

Poor hearing

It's quite common for young children to have something called 'glue ear', which is a condition that can occur after a cold or flu, when the tubes inside the ear become blocked. It's only temporary but it means that hearing is affected. When children can't hear properly they can easily lose concentration, especially in class. Inattentiveness can be put down to bad behaviour, rather than a physical problem. It's a good idea to tell the teacher if you are concerned about your child's hearing

> Cut down on any background noise while you are working together – even the hum of a computer can muffle the sound of someone's voice.

Other concerns

There are two conditions that everyone is talking about these days.

Dyslexia

> Dyslexia is a word that comes from Greek meaning 'difficulty with words'.

A child with dyslexia has particular trouble with reading and spelling, and may write letters back to front. These are just two clues that suggest a child might be dyslexic. You can find out more about it here: www.bdadyslexia.org.uk/aboutdyslexia.html

ADHD

> ADHD stands for attention-deficit hyperactivity disorder.

A child with ADHD is restless and overactive, chatters a lot and finds it very hard to concentrate for long. Again these are just a few of the possible signs. You can find out more about it here:

www.rcpsych.ac.uk/mentalhealthinformation/mentalhealth
andgrowingup/5adhdhyperkineticdisorder.aspx

⚠ **Warning** Many children have difficulty with reading or are restless who do NOT have dyslexia or ADHD! Some people may use these terms incorrectly to excuse poor spelling or bad behaviour.

Specialist help is needed if you suspect your child has either of these conditions or if one of these is diagnosed in your child.

Literacy in schools today

The Primary National Strategy

Way back in 1997, the government launched the **National Literacy Strategy**, with the aim of raising standards in English primary schools. Since then the policy has been reviewed and developed. In 2005, literacy became part of the **Primary National Strategy** along with numeracy.

The **Primary National Strategy** is statutory in England. In Wales, some areas choose to follow it. In Scotland and Northern Ireland the education systems are different.

If you're really keen, you can look online and see exactly what every primary school teacher uses in order to plan literacy and numeracy lessons throughout your child's primary school career. This is called the **Primary Framework** and can be found here: www.standards.dfes.gov.uk/primaryframework/

It sets out clearly what pupils should be taught in each term of their time in primary school. The idea is that every child has an equal chance because each one is given the opportunity to learn the same things in the same order. It helps teachers to make sure that everything is covered. It tells teachers *what* to teach, but they are left to decide *how* to teach it, depending on the individual needs of the children in their class.

If you do take a look at the Primary Framework, don't panic! There are lots of technical words used that might throw you into confusion and make you think that you'll never be able to help your child because it's far too complicated. That's exactly why this book has been written. It will explain many of the words you may come across when helping your child with literacy. Look at page 75 for the jargon-busting glossary of terms.

Twelve 'strands of learning' have been identified in order to make things easier to follow.

THE TWELVE STRANDS

Speak and listen for a wide range of purposes in different contexts:

1. speaking

2. listening and responding

3. group discussion and interaction

4. drama

Read and write for a range of purposes on paper and on screen:

5. word recognition: decoding (reading) and encoding (spelling)

6. word structure and spelling

7. understanding and interpreting texts

8. engaging and responding to texts

9. creating and shaping texts

10. text structure and organization

11. sentence structure and punctuation

12. presentation.

Remember, you know your child better than anyone else, and you are the person who can make the most difference.

Teachers are required to teach literacy for five hours per week. In the early days of the Literacy Strategy, this took the form of a very structured daily Literacy Hour. Lately the approach has become more relaxed, but the same ideas are still used.

Each lesson will be a combination of the following parts:

- The teacher explains the purpose of the lesson.

- Shared work.

  - The teacher demonstrates a skill and the children watch and learn.

- Guided work.

  - In small groups, the skill is put into practice, with pupils given the support they need to be successful.

- Independent work.

  - A pupil has the confidence to work alone using the newly mastered skill.

- The plenary.

  - The whole class discusses the lesson and celebrates success.

Use this as a guide for yourself when working with your child – demonstrating, helping a lot, helping less, then not helping at all, but still being there to encourage and congratulate.

Overall, for literacy, there will be a mixture of word, sentence and text level work.

Word level:

■ Words on their own, not as part of a sentence.

■ How to spell the words.

■ What the words mean.

Sentence level:

■ How to build up a sentence.

■ Punctuation.

■ Grammar.

■ Paragraphs.

■ Style.

Text level:

■ Different sorts of texts, for example:

• plays, stories, poems, diaries, newspaper articles.

■ Different forms of writing, for example:

• to inform, persuade, entertain.

Key Stage 2

Pupils who are 7 to 11 years old are said to be at Key Stage 2. At school, Key Stage 2 children are in Years 3, 4, 5 and 6.

To measure your child's progress at school, each subject is divided into different levels. English, taught at primary schools using the framework set out in the Primary National Strategy, has eight levels.

An average ability child is expected to have gained Level 4 at the end of Key Stage 2. See Appendix 1 on page 71 if you want to see some of the levels for reading and writing.

Please remember that the levels are only a rough guide. All children are different and progress at different rates. If your child has special educational needs, these levels are not helpful. What is important for *all* children is that *progress is being made*, not that your child is at the 'right' level.

SATs

SATs are the national assessment tests taken by pupils in Year 6, at the end of Key Stage 2. They cover the three core subjects – English, maths and science – and take place in May. At Key Stage 2 they are more formal than at Key Stage 1.

 SATs stands for Standard Assessment Tasks.

Teachers are under a lot of pressure because the overall SAT scores in a school determine its position in the national league tables. These have been created by the government with the idea that they will tell us which school is 'the best' so of course there is a tendency to 'drill' pupils so that they achieve the best possible results.

A new idea has been announced by the government, which is to replace SATs with tests tailored to the needs of each child rather than everybody doing the same test on the same day. Teachers generally agree that this would be much better. The new idea might be put in place in 2010, but until it happens there will be SATs!

Should you, as a parent or carer, worry about SATs? Should you spend a fortune buying all those work books then make your child battle through them? No you shouldn't! SATs are simply checks to see how much your child has learned, mainly for the purpose of government statistics. They are not something your child can pass or fail.

Concentrate instead on making sure that your child is not put under 'exam pressure' at such a young age. That will happen all too soon in secondary school.

Literacy at home

Speaking and listening

It's good to talk . . . and listen!

The first four literacy strands are closely related to those you'll find set out in the National Curriculum for English.

- **Speaking:** being able to speak clearly and develop and sustain ideas in talk.

- **Listening:** developing active listening strategies and critical skills of analysis.

- **Group discussion and interaction:** taking different roles in groups, making a range of contributions and working collaboratively.

- **Drama:** improvising and working in role, scripting and performing, and responding to performances.

Surprised? No reading or writing involved, but it still comes under the umbrella of literacy. It's still taught in school. See Table 1 for examples.

It all seems a bit vague as a teaching area. With reading and writing there's something to focus on – a book to work your way through, or a story to complete. It's clear what your child is doing and how you can help. It's also easy to see where progress is being made, or to spot areas where extra support might be needed.

Speaking and listening, on the other hand . . . how on earth do you help with those? Why are speaking and listening things that need to be taught anyway? Your child can already do them, can't he?

Table 1. Examples of teaching objectives for speaking and listening

Strand	Year 3 Term 2
Speaking	To choose and prepare poems or stories for performance, identifying appropriate expression, tone, volume and use of voices and other sounds
Listening	To identify the presentational features used to communicate the main points in a broadcast
Group discussion and interaction	To actively include and respond to all members of the group
Drama	To identify and discuss qualities of others' performances, including gesture, action and costume

Strand	Year 4 Term 1
Speaking	To use and reflect on some ground rules for dialogue
Listening	To compare the different contributions of music, words and images in short extracts from TV programmes
Group discussion and interaction	To take different roles in groups and use language appropriate to them, including the roles of leader, reporter, scribeor mentor
Drama	To comment constructively on plays and performance, discussing effects and how they are achieved

Strand	Year 5 Term 3
Speaking	To present a spoken argument, sequencing points logically, defending views with evidence and making use of persuasive language
Listening	To analyse the use of persuasive language
Group discussion and interaction	To understand different ways to take the lead and support others in groups
Drama	To use and recognize the impact of theatrical effects in drama

Strand	Year 6 Term 1
Speaking	To use techniques of dialogic talk to explore ideas, topics or issues
Listening	To listen for language variation in formal and informal contexts
Group discussion and interaction	To identify the ways spoken language varies according to differences in context and purpose of use
Drama	To devise a performance considering how to adapt the performance for a specific audience

Here's the answer!

For most children, talking is a lot easier than writing. It's an opportunity to try out different ways of putting words and sentences together without having to master the skills needed to put pen to paper. A child will learn the art of speaking through listening – listening to **you** above all, as his parent or carer – listening to the words you use and how you adjust the way you speak depending on who it is you are talking to.

You can help your child more than you ever thought possible simply by talking to her in a range of ways that will be good examples for her to copy.

You can help your child by encouraging her to listen as well.

Group discussion and interaction is what happens in your family every day when your son wants fishfingers for tea but your daughter wants spaghetti hoops. Or dad would like to watch the football on the TV but mum prefers a soap opera.

This is a perfect opportunity for a discussion; listening to another person's point of view; weighing up the argument on each side; negotiating and coming to a decision together. This is known as **dialogue.**

For the sake of family harmony, dialogue is a lot more constructive than the 'whoever shouts loudest wins' approach as well!

Drama is probably more relevant to the classroom, but there are certainly some activities you could have fun with at home or as an outing.

Going to the theatre can be expensive, but sometimes local amateur dramatics societies put on performances that are suitable for children – and not just pantomimes.

Seeing a live show together is a not-to-be-missed opportunity for both of you.

Putting on a live show for doting grandparents is something that your child may love to do at home as well, even if the thought fills you with horror! If space is limited, a puppet show would work just as well. You don't need a puppet theatre – behind the sofa is a perfect place for children to conceal themselves, with puppets performing along the top. Making puppets can be fun, but even that isn't necessary. Soft toys or plastic figures from your child's toy box would work just as well.

If you're feeling a bit more ambitious, here is a website which tells you all about making a shadow puppet theatre from a cardboard box – a great rainy day activity: www.molli.org.uk/burma/theatre/make.htm

The good news!

The wonderful thing about speaking and listening is that you and your child can learn together while waiting for the bus, walking to school, going on a long car journey, shopping, eating tea, even watching television . . . you don't have to set aside a special time for it.

> **⚠ Warning** Remember, speaking and listening go on all the time, but in order to make them valuable for your child, you might have to do a little bit of planning!

If there is **one** thing that you could do which would make a big difference it would be this: use fewer **closed questions** and more **open questions** when talking to your child.

It's easy to see that if you use open questions it will give your child much more practice with listening, thinking and

? A *closed question* can be answered with a single word or a short phrase, e.g. 'What colour is that?', 'How old are you?', 'Are you hot?'

An *open question* invites a longer answer, e.g. 'Why do you think he did that?', 'How are you feeling?', 'What shall we do next?'

putting together a longer response. It will also provide a model for him to copy when he's asking questions himself.

TV or not TV?

Yes there's some rubbish on TV, but your child needs to relax sometimes! You can't fight it, so why not use it? Make time to sit down with him. There must be *something* you would both enjoy! Talk about the programme while it's on. Discuss it afterwards. Practise your open questions ('Why did she do that?' 'What do you think will happen in the next episode?').

Here's one of the teaching objectives from the drama strand: 'Identify and discuss qualities of others' performances, including gesture, action, costume'. Ideal discussion material when you're watching TV.

Following are some more ideas to get you started with speaking and listening.

The good ideas bank!

■ **A cunning plan!** *To use talk to organize roles and action.* Make a pizza, make a cake, whatever you decide. Talk through every stage of the process together – assembling the ingredients, selecting the kitchen equipment. What do you think we should do next? Why are you using that bowl?

- **Startling stories.** *To tell stories using voice effectively.* Choose a story that you both know well. Try out different voices for each character. You could each take on a few roles. Then tell the story together. You could even test it out on a younger brother or sister.

- **Tell me how!** *To explain a process or present information.* Pretend that you're a visitor from another planet. Ask your child to give you instructions to carry out a simple task, e.g. cleaning teeth, making a cup of tea. Do EXACTLY what she says. She'll soon realize the need for accuracy! Now reverse roles.

- **Greetings cards.** *To investigate how talk varies with familiarity.* Collect pictures of different people – family members, the Queen, a doctor, babies, children, a judge, shop assistants. Look at them together and decide how you'd say hello to them, ask a question. What would you talk about? What's the difference and why? Introduce the idea of **formal and informal language** and their different uses.

(?) *Formal language* is most often used between people who don't know each other very well. Complete sentences and precise vocabulary are generally used. Phrases are linked by words such as 'however' and 'therefore'.

Informal language is most often used between friends and family members. Sentences are often incomplete (e.g. Sounds great! Could do!) and words are replaced with more casual ones (e.g. Yep or yeah or OK for yes).

- **Listen here!** *To listen for language variation in formal and informal contexts.* Now that you've sorted that out, next time you're watching TV together or listening to the radio, you can pick out examples of informal and formal language. Tell your child you've forgotten the difference and ask if she can help you.

- **Listen here too.** *To investigate how talk varies with age, gender and purpose.* Listen to talk programmes on the radio. Together, identify the speakers: male or female? Old or young? Why are they speaking? (Reading the news, telling jokes, advertising something, making a speech and so on.) How can you tell the difference?

- **What's up?** *To use and reflect on some ground rules for dialogue.* Have some fun with a conversation! Your child has to spot what's wrong with the way you're going about it. Speak too quietly/loudly/fast/slowly. When your child talks, put your hands over your ears or turn up the radio. Afterwards you can discuss what makes a conversation work.

- **Family conference.** *To present a spoken argument, sequencing points logically, defending views with evidence and making use of persuasive language.* Maybe you have some sort of issue to sort out, such as what is a reasonable bedtime or who should clean out the hamster cage? It happens all the time in families. Use it! Decide on a time when you can all sit down together. Give your child time to present her case.

Prepare your argument as well. Listen to each other. Come to a compromise.

■ **Knowing me, knowing you.** *To create roles showing how behaviour can be interpreted from different viewpoints.* You could swap places with your child, for fun. Allow him to try to get you off to bed, or eat some vegetables. It should be a valuable experience for both of you!

That's speaking and listening! Thoughtfully developed, using some of the ideas above, (or your own even better ones) it will provide a wonderful foundation for improving reading and writing skills.

The rest of the literacy strands (5–12) are about reading and writing. It's important to remember that speaking and listening, reading and writing all support each other. Although, in this book, they are dealt with in different sections, they work as a team in your child's daily life.

Children try out ideas in talk before they write them down, but writing can help to organize thoughts more easily so speech is less muddled.

Children generally talk before they read but reading a book aloud will help a child learn speech patterns that they can use for themselves later on.

Talking about reading . . . that's the next section!

Reading

Been there, done that!

'My child has been at school for more than three years. She doesn't need my help any more. She seems to be able to read quite well now, and the rest will just come with time, won't it?'

It might but in very many cases it might not, and it's simply not worth the risk. Withdrawing your support too early is a bit like removing the stabilizers from her bike before she can balance properly. It *could* work but, on the other hand, it could at the very least slow down her progress or, much worse, destroy the confidence you have helped her to build up over the years.

Reading is a complicated process, with many strategies that need to be mastered. In the early stages of learning, a child can get away with relying on one or two parts of the process, such as using pictures to help her or understanding phonics. As she gets older, she'll be expected to read more advanced material and will need to pull together all her skills in order to be able to read independently and effectively.

Let's go back to basics.

Reading refresher

It is widely accepted that the most successful approach to reading is to use a whole range of strategies. Most of the time you don't even realize what you're doing. It's something that comes to you, as an adult, automatically. Children need to learn what these strategies are, then if one way doesn't work for them they can use another instead.

> ⚠️ **Warning** **What works for you might not work for your child! Things have moved on since you were at school. There is no one right way to learn to read!**

Reading strategies

Knowing about the context

If you know what the book is about then you will also have a good idea of what the words might say.

Pictures, on the cover and on the pages inside the book, can be a great help too.

A quickie! Grab a pile of books and see if you can predict what they're about just by looking at the cover. You might also be able to tell which age group they're aimed at by the style of the pictures. They could be fiction or factual books.

Warning Guessing the words written under a picture might be successful but to be sure the guess is correct other evidence is needed.

The girl runs away from the dog.

Knowing about phonics

Phonics is the study of the links between letters and sounds. We see the letter P, for example, and know the sound it makes when we say it. We hear the sound P and know that we use the letter P to write it.

In school, *analytical phonics* might be used.

? *Analytical phonics* makes use of each *letter* to build up a word. 'Shop' would be built up from /s/ /h/ /o/ and /p/.

Recently, *synthetic phonics* has become popular.

(?) *Synthetic phonics* **builds up words from its separate sounds. 'Shop' in this case, would be built up from the sounds /sh/ and /o/ and /p/.**

If your child sounds out an unfamiliar word, she's using phonics to help her.

To use phonics, of course, you need to know the 26 letters of the alphabet and the sounds they make. It's much more useful to know the *sound* than the name of the letter. For example, if you want to spell the word 'hot' it is so much easier when you say /h/ (not aitch) /o/ (not owe) and /t/ (not tee).

In the English language there are 44 *sounds* that we use when we talk, which can be single letters or can be made up of two or three letters in combination, such as the sounds /ch/ and /igh/. These sounds are called *phonemes* and when we write a phoneme down, the letter or letter combination we use is called a *grapheme*. See Tables 2 and 3 for lists of these phonemes.

In addition, two letters that make up one sound are called *digraphs* (such as /ch/) and three letters that make up one sound are called *trigraphs* (like /igh/)

When you join phonemes (or graphemes) together to make a word, or a bigger chunk of a word, it's called *blending.* For example, you blend /th/ and /r/ and /ee/ to make the word 'three'.

(?) **A** *digraph* **such as /sh/ has only one sound. A** *blend* **such as /st/ is the sound /s/ and the sound /t/ run together.**

Table 2. Vowel phonemes

A vowel is a sound made by changing the shape of your mouth when air comes out.

A E I O and U are vowels, and Y can be sometimes (e.g. in happy but not in yes).

Phoneme examples:

a	rat				
e	set	head			
i	hip	waited			
o	cog	want			
u	rug	love			
ae	rain	stay	plate	nation	
ee	feet	please	belief	these	
ie	denied	sight	why	fine	kind
oe	toad	show	alone	sold	
ue	soon	true	knew	dune	
oo	cook	should	put		
ar	start	path*(regional)			
ur	turn	dirty	herd	learn	work
or	born	floor	war		
au	naughty	saw	tall		
er	happen	circle	teacher		
ow	clown	out			
oi	soil	toy			
air	fair	bear	share		
ear	clear	steer	here		

*In the north of England, for example, words such as path would use an /a/ sound as in 'cat'.

In these tables, you can see that there are sometimes several ways to spell one sound – that is to say several graphemes might correspond to one phoneme.

Table 3. Consonant phonemes

A consonant is a sound and the letter that represents it. You use part of your mouth to alter the sound. For example, when you say /p/ you use your lips, when you say /f/ you use your teeth on your lips.

Phoneme examples:

b	**b**oot			
d	**d**ish			
f	**f**rog	**ph**one		
g	**g**ood			
h	**h**and			
j	ju**dge**	**g**iraffe	char**ge**	
k	**c**oo**k**	qui**ck**ly	si**x**	**ch**ronic
l	**l**ost			
m	**m**other	la**mb**		
n	**n**ote	**kn**ot	**gn**ome	
p	**p**erson			
r	**r**oof	**wr**inkle		
s	**s**ort	cha**s**e	**c**eiling	s**c**ience
t	**t**iny			
v	**v**ehicle			
w	**w**asp			
wh	**wh**y			
y	**y**ellow			
z	**z**ebra	the**s**e	**s**	
th	**th**ere			
th	**th**ick			
ch	**ch**eek	ca**tch**		
sh	**sh**elter	na**ti**on	mi**ss**ion	ten**si**on **ch**ef
zh	plea**s**ure			
ng	bri**ng**	thi**n**k		

When you're sounding out words that contain blends, it's best to sound out the combinations as one unit – for instance sc-a-n not s-c-a-n – because it will help so much with your child's reading fluency and spelling.

In this short section alone, you can probably see very clearly how reading, writing and spelling are all interlinked.

Knowing about grammar

Grammar means a lot more than learning about the different parts of a sentence – the nouns, the verbs the adjectives and so on – although that is part of it.

See the Glossary on page 75 for an explanation of the main grammatical terms. There's a very useful website too: www.grammaticallycorrect.co.uk/

Grammatical knowledge means:

- knowing the rules about words and how to put them together in phrases, sentences and longer pieces of text;

- understanding how words and language patterns are used to convey meaning in a particular way.

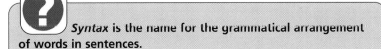 **Syntax** is the name for the grammatical arrangement of words in sentences.

If you can help your child develop these skills, then, when he is reading something tricky, he'll be able to predict what a word might say, even if he doesn't recognize it. He'll know which types of words are used where, and what makes sense and what doesn't.

Of course, this knowledge comes first and foremost by listening to people talking!

Reading is not just being able to recognize words: it's about being able to make sense of them too. Your child may be familiar with a word on its own, but in a sentence it takes its full meaning from the other words that are there as well.

An adjective on its own doesn't do much of a job! It only has a real purpose if it's together with a noun. Take the word 'tiny' – you know what it means; your child knows what it means too, but it's only when it's put next to another word such as 'dog' that a picture is painted in your mind. A tiny dog!

? An *adjective* is a word that modifies the meaning of a *noun* by describing it (*pretty, red*) identifying it (*my, your*) or quantifying it (*many, few, all*).

? A *noun* is a word used to name a person, animal, place, thing or abstract idea – *Charlie, horse, garden, ironing-board* and *prayer* are all nouns.

Charlie is a *proper noun* – the name of a specific person, so is written with a capital letter, as is a place name such as London.

Take a look at this sentence:

'Jack licked his lips greedily when he saw the huge pie in front of him.'

Imagine that your child isn't familiar with the word *greedily.* How can he, using grammatical knowledge, make a good attempt to guess what it might be?

- He sees that the word must be an adverb, partly because it ends in -ly and partly because it adds meaning to the verb phrase 'licked his lips'.

- He understands the sense of the rest of the sentence. If you lick your lips at the sight of a huge pie, it's a safe guess you're greedy!

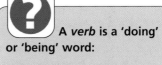

? An *adverb* modifies the meaning of a *verb* and often ends in -ly: *quickly, sadly, unfortunately*.

? A *verb* is a 'doing' or 'being' word:

Amir *jumps* over the fence.
Ellie *was* in the garden.

With those clues, he can then bring his knowledge of phonics into play as well, in order to recognize the word on its own. Then he can read the whole sentence to see if the word greedily makes sense in that place. Success!

Knowing about words

Young children learn to recognize simple words by sight. They see the word *book* and they don't have to use phonics or grammatical knowledge or picture clues to know that it says *book*. As time goes by, they gradually build up a bank of words in their mind so more and more will come easily to them when they're reading.

This skill can be developed still further when a child can use her experience of one word to help her with another unfamiliar word.

Your child knows the word *book*. She knows the word *shop*. She see a new word when she's reading – *bookshop*. Panic! Maybe at first. Then, if she calms down and thinks to herself, 'I know the first half of the word says *book*, I know the second half says *shop* … that's it! *Bookshop*!' She can then check to see if that word makes sense in the sentence. Success again!

Developing still further, an older child will learn the meaning of different parts of words and be able to apply that knowledge to other words she hasn't seen before.

Take the word *unable*. Your child is *unable* to recognize it when she's reading it BUT she knows the word *able* and she knows that *un* changes the meaning to a negative – so, putting that knowledge together, she has it! No longer *unable* to make sense of the word *unable*!

? The smallest unit of meaning in a word is called a *morpheme*. A word can contain more than one morpheme.

As we've seen with the word *unable*, it can be broken down into two morphemes: *able* and *un-* to make it negative. The word *bungalow* is only one morpheme. It cannot be broken down into smaller units of meaning.

It's that sort of logical thinking that you can help your child with when you're reading together.

Don't forget to supply your child with a dictionary so she can look up unfamiliar words. See page 67 for a list of suitable ones.

Your understanding of *all* the reading strategies will enable you to be a wonderful reading partner for your child.

Keep talking about it! Don't just be pleased that your child has succeeded in reading a new word that was causing him problems. Discuss together *how* he managed it. That will make sure that the strategies are firmly fixed in his mind even when you're not around to help him.

More than knowing how to do it!

In some cases, particularly with boys, it's not so much a case of *how* to read, but of somehow getting a child to do it at all!

That's where you, as a parent or carer, really come into your own. It's not easy when reading has to compete with PlayStations, TV, computer games and iPods.

Here's the good news: reading doesn't just include books! If you're in despair about your child's reluctance, then spend a little time thinking of all the things he *does* read – comics, road signs, cereal packets, instructions for that new electronic gadget, shopping lists, words on the computer screen, toy catalogues, text on the TV . . .

Ian Rankin, a well-known author who writes the Rebus crime novels, thinks that poor literacy among boys has a lot to do with the lack of comics on sale these days. That was what started him off with his reading when he was young. There *are* comics on sale, and comic-style books, such as the *Asterix* and *TinTin* series. With far fewer words and plenty of exciting pictures, they are much less demanding to read and great fun too.

Warning Look out for comics in newsagents, but check them for content before you buy them. Some can be unsuitable for young children.

Reading is not just for pleasure. It can have a purpose too – to find out some information, to be told how to carry out a task, to be warned that something is dangerous . . .

When your child brings notes home from school, sit down and get him to read it out to you. It is about his world, after all!

Think creatively and make reading something that's fun, worthwhile and essential. Computers can and should be used to read for information. Lead by example. If your child never sees you reading, then he won't see the need to bother with it himself.

At school, he will be expected to write reports, formal letters, persuasive arguments, newspaper articles ... all sorts of different forms of writing. How will he be able to choose the right language to use and the correct layout if he's never read anything like this himself?

The very best thing you can do is provide a huge variety of reading matter for your child – magazines, newspapers, information leaflets, instructions, letters, posters, flyers – you name it, it will help your child in the future to read it now!

Don't shy away from books, either. A library isn't full of stuffy old volumes covered in dust – it's like an Aladdin's Cave full of excitement – shelves of brightly coloured books on every subject you could possibly imagine. Libraries are free!

Buying books can be costly but a well-loved book is read over and over again so you could say it's good value. Going to bookshops, choosing books, can be an enjoyable outing and may be a hidden learning opportunity too.

Your child may be attracted to a book first of all by the picture on the cover, but reading the title and looking inside and sampling some of the text, will provide extra practice. It will also develop your child's ability to assess reading material and make decisions.

Buying online is another way to go about it, but make sure you're there when books are purchased in this way! There are plenty of websites but, if you need help to find suitable book choices, Richard and Judy, from the TV, have an online book club with a section devoted to children. It's very helpful as a guide for selecting books for children of different ages, if you're not sure.

The site has lots of advice and activities for children too: www.richardandjudybookclub.co.uk

 A book for every occasion!

Are you going on a day trip or on holiday together? Has your child suddenly become interested in horses, or skate-boarding or hip-hop? Is he wondering how on earth aeroplanes stay up in the sky? Then go to the library together and find a book about it!

Bedtime stories

Too old now? Not at all. Why not read a page each? Or get your child to read YOU a bedtime story, perhaps one she has written herself! Or she could read to a younger brother or sister, but make sure you're there too, to encourage her.

Treasure hunt

Make your child work for a reward (but in a fun way).
Write a set of clues that he has to follow and at the end he
will have his prize. He *will* stay up half an hour later to
watch the football, or have an extra game on his
PlayStation or whatever you know will be a good incentive.

Use that computer!

There are some great websites that will help your child –
and to children, computers seem more like good fun and
less like work. Check out the BBC Schools website. Each
activity is marked with an age range to help you out. Here's
just one address to get you started:
www.bbc.co.uk/schools/ks2bitesize/english/

Helping hands

Do you need to assemble some flat-pack furniture? Or use a
recipe to make the dinner? Your child can be your assistant
and read out the instructions for you.

Sign language

There are signs everywhere – in the supermarket, on the
motorway, on the street. When you're out and about, use
the opportunity to practise together.

Simon says!

Remember that game you used
to play at children's parties? You
could make it into a reading
exercise, by writing down tasks
for your child to carry out. Make
them silly – *'Simon says balance
a pea on your nose'* – or make
them useful – *'Simon says tidy
your bedroom.'* The first idea
will probably be more popular!

Reading for relevance

Children may research on the internet when they need to find something out for a school project, or when they have to write a factual essay. It's a common problem, and all too easy, for a child to 'cut and paste' a whole section of information without reading it thoroughly to make sure it really is relevant.

Using a computer, you could make up a document that mixes up two sets of information (about space rockets and knitting, for example). Your child could read through and sort out which paragraphs belong to which subject.

Writing

The right way to write

One day there might come a time when using a word processor on a computer will do away with the need to write by hand, but that time hasn't arrived yet!

Schools generally have a hand-writing policy – a particular style that they use – so it's worth checking that out before you work with your child. One thing that won't be different is the correct way to hold a pencil or pen.

This *is* important, even if you think your child has quite good writing when he holds a pen incorrectly. It might slow him up badly and even cause him pain if he has to write for long periods. It's important, too, that he can write quickly, because there's more and more writing to do the further he progresses through school.

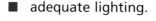 **Check back to page 8 for information about how to help left-handed children.**

You can't write for him, but you can do lots of things to make sure it's as easy as possible by providing:

- suitable writing tools – splodgy ball point pens and blunt pencils won't help!

- a clear space to work on

- a sensible chair that's the right height for the desk or table

- adequate lighting.

Knowing how to form individual letters is vital but, at this stage, joining up letters efficiently is what needs most practice. This is called *cursive writing*.

Cursive writing is joined-up writing. *Printing* means writing each letter individually and is much slower.

A younger child might use ENORMOUS letters when writing, but by now your child's writing should be smaller with

- size and spacing of letters consistent

- letters sitting on the line.

Having learned to write in a particular style, children may now develop a personal style. Whatever it is, it's fine as long as it's confident, flowing and, most important of all, legible.

For every bit of school work, not just literacy, it's important that your child's handwriting is legible. Unless it is, no-one will be able to see how clever he is!

> ⚠ **Warning** Set aside a special time to practise handwriting and ONLY handwriting. Don't try to correct spelling mistakes or other errors at the same time.

Writing and computers

There's no getting away from it – using computers is an important means of developing language in the context of the modern world.

Just as your child sometimes uses calculators and sometimes mental arithmetic for maths, she should be given the opportunity to use a keyboard to write with as well as a pen and paper.

If you have a computer at home then put it to good use. Libraries often have computers too, if not.

> ⚠ **Warning** This book isn't a computer guide, so you may have to find an expert if you're stuck. What's the betting that your child will know how to do everything anyway, exactly as she can use the remote control to record a TV programme when you haven't a clue how to do it!

Here are some things that might be useful:

- ■ Write something directly on screen.

- ■ Use word processing techniques (such as deleting, cutting and pasting) to develop writing skills.

- ■ Use a range of fonts and layouts when writing for different audiences and purposes.

- ■ Use grammar and spellcheckers to make sure work is accurate.

Fiction for fun!

The fiction section of literacy includes stories, poetry and plays. For boys, it is generally true to say that this is more difficult to encourage than non-fiction. Sad to say, they often consider it to be 'too girlie'. It's up to you to convince them otherwise!

There's no easy solution, for boys and girls alike. At school, children will be expected to produce some extended pieces of writing. You might not be able to help with the whole thing, but what you *can* do is offer support with different skills that are required. Added together, these will allow your child to create something that is more exciting, more colourful and more entertaining to read. It's rather like providing all the ingredients so that your child can bake a tasty cake!

None of the activities below need be written, but they *will* help with more imaginative writing. Your child could keep a book such as a dictionary of all the exciting words you think up. Then she could use them when she writes her next story.

Here are some ideas that might trigger off something in your own mind.

Wacky words!

Choose a simple word – it could be an adjective such as *small*, an adverb such as *quietly*, or verb such as *to walk*. These are all dull, dull, DULL! List other words that could replace them and be more exciting. *Tiny, tiddly, minuscule – on tip-toes, softly, faintly – stroll, totter, march . . .*

 A *synonym* is a word that means the same as another.

Smiley similes!

Make up some exciting similes! You could start them off and your child could finish them. *'As wobbly as a . . .' As slippery as a . . .' 'He ran like a . . .'*

A *simile* is a comparison between two different things. 'Her hands were as cold as ice.' 'His hair shone like gold.'

Magic metaphors

Make up some metaphors too!

A *metaphor* is like a simile but instead of saying one thing is *like* another, you say it *is* something else. 'You are my sunshine.' 'The world is a stage.'

Sound series

It's fun if you make up sentences using words that start with the same letter. This is called *alliteration* and is often to be found in poetry. *Pretty Penny painted Peter's paper.* Thinking of these series of words is a great help with phonics too.

Alliteration is a series of words that start with the same sound.

Sounds like . . .

Some words sound like their meaning: *cuckoo, hiss, sizzle, bubble.* Look out for them; use them! This is called *onomatopoeia.*

> **?** *Onomatopoeia* is the use of a word that sounds like its meaning: *swish, smack.*

Exciting writing

You've helped your child to build up a whole new vocabulary of interesting words, now it's time to put them to good use. Unleash his creative skills!

> **⚠ Warning** There are lots of things to think about when writing – such as spelling and punctuation. Sometimes it's important for your child to be able to write freely without worrying about these things. If you spend all your time working on the nitty-gritty details, then *of course* writing won't be something that your child looks forward to. Come to an agreement. 'Today we're not going to worry about spelling. We just want to think about a really exciting story.' Another day, you could look at the story already written and work on the spelling.

Perhaps he likes writing stories, in which case you're laughing, but maybe he doesn't. Here are some ideas that might, just might, set him on his way to write with enjoyment.

Write

■ An episode of a favourite TV programme.

■ A story with sound effects. Collect all the things needed to make the noises.

■ A bedtime story for a little brother or sister.

■ A story using favourite characters such as Indiana Jones or Buffy the Vampire Slayer.

■ A ghost story, then read it by torchlight.

■ A murder mystery, then make it into a game to guess whodunnit.

Or

■ Have you got a camcorder? Your child could write a script then film it! If not, write a play script and get some friends together to perform it to an audience. Or both!

- Design a robot or a super hero.

- Choose three objects and write a story with each of them in it.

- Take a well-known story, such as Little Red Riding Hood, and write a different ending.

Or

. . . if your child is really stuck, and can't think of a single idea, help her like this

There are four main elements that make up a story:

- characters (the people or animals or other creatures in the story)

- the place (the setting)

- the situation (an event which starts off the action)

- objects (things that the characters use).

Use one box for each element. Together, write down interesting examples of each on pieces of paper.

Interesting characters – a goblin with one leg; a pirate who is frightened of water; the cleverest horse in the world.

Interesting places – in a kingdom under the sea; on a wibbly-wobbly bridge; at the North Pole.

Interesting situations – the sun has disappeared; you go to school and there's no-one there; all the animals have escaped from a zoo.

Interesting objects – a bucket full of snakes; a superman costume; a magic broomstick.

When you have enough, pick an example or two from each box. There you have the start of an exciting story.

Poetry please

The thought of writing poetry might send a chill right through you, but children are far less worried about this skill than adults. Poetry doesn't have to be serious and literary. It can be fun. Just to prove it:

My granny came to visit

My granny came to visit
She stayed for half a day
She ate up all the biscuits
And threw the tin away

She scribbled on a cupboard
And spilt a cup of tea
And mum was very angry,
Not with granny, but with ME!

She said . . .

'How could you be so naughty?
I don't know what to say!'

And granny stuck her tongue out
And went outside to play.

There is a great website at www.poetry4kids.com It will liven up your day and give you and your child some inspiration!

Sometimes children can find that writing poetry is a useful way to express feelings that are difficult to talk about. Here is an extract from a poem by a 10-year-old boy, written when his grandfather died. He jotted down all his thoughts and memories, then organized them into a poem.

I'm not sure about Grandad

Even when I was very small
I would run against grandad down the road.
I'm not sure if he let me win.

I liked helping him in the garage
Taking things apart and fixing things.
I'm not sure if I was really helping.

Grandad collected everything old
Cameras, binoculars, technology things.
I'm not sure if they were really useful.

When I last saw him, grandad was skinny and quiet
But his moustache was still bristly.
I'm not sure if I liked seeing him like that.

It was quite good that he died
Because he was so ill, but
I'm not sure if it was the best thing.

Laurie Coxon

You can see from these two examples that poems can be:

■ fun or serious

■ long or short

■ rhyming or without rhyme.

There are different types of poems. Here are some that your child might learn about at school.

Haiku

Haiku is a type of poem that came originally from Japan. It has 17 syllables, divided into three lines – 5–7–5. Traditionally a haiku is about nature.

> **?** A *syllable* is a chunk of sound in a word. *Hat* has one syllable, *table* has two, and *bicycle* has three.

Here is an example of haiku with the syllables marked in afterwards.

Autumn leaf

Curled paper canoe
It floats in the misty dawn
Light as a feather

Curled paper canoe
  1 **2 3** **4 5**

It floats in the misty dawn
1 **2** **3** **4** **5 6** **7**

Light as a feather
  1 **2 3 4 5**

Shape (or concrete) poem

As its name suggests, this type of poem is written in the shape of its subject.

Lightning

Zig-zagging across the night,

jagged lightning

cuts through the sky.

Acrostic

An acrostic is a poetic form which uses the initial letters of a key word.

Take the word '*sun*'.

Sun

Shining golden bright

Up in the clear blue sky

No clouds hiding its light.

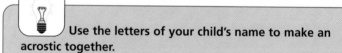

Use the letters of your child's name to make an acrostic together.

Kenning

A kenning is a bit like a riddle and was used in ancient Norse and Celtic writing. It uses two-word phrases to describe an object. A dog, for example, could be described as a 'stick-chaser' or 'tail-wagger'. It's simple and good fun to put together kennings, which often appear in the form of a list. A very well-known advert for a fizzy drink is a kenning – 'lip-smackin' thirst-quenchin' ace-tastin' . . .'

Fish

Tail-swishing

Fin-flapping

Eye-goggling

Bubble-making

Water-slicer

Limerick

A limerick is a five-line poem with a very strict rhyme and form. Edward Lear was a nonsense poet who made them popular in the nineteenth century. They are often funny, and some are rude!

There was a young lady from Brighton
Who slept every night with the light on
'It's the monsters,' she said,
'living under my bed.'
This cowardly lady from Brighton.

Don't let poetry frighten you. It can be so much fun for you and your child.

As we've already discussed, writing is not just used to entertain or as a way of being creative, it's also used for more serious reasons.

Actual factual writing

There are six types of factual text used in school that your child will be expected to master:

Recount

Retells events in time order – for example, an account of a school trip or a holiday, an event in history, a diary.

Report

Gives factual information about a specific topic – for example, a holiday brochure, an information leaflet, a magazine article, an encyclopaedia entry.

Instruction

Tells us how to do something – for example, a recipe for a cake, how to make a kite, how to conduct a science experiment or play a board game.

Explanation

Tells us how or why something happens – for example, there are often explanations in geography, science and history books.

Persuasion

Tells us why we should think something (from one viewpoint) – for example, advertisements, a politician's speech, a campaign brochure.

Discussion

Presents arguments from differing viewpoints – for example, a balanced newspaper article, minutes from a debate.

As we discussed in the reading section, if your child sees and reads all these different texts, then she will have much less difficulty when she comes to write them, because she'll know what is expected.

Each text type has certain features that single it out from the others. The Lancashire Grid for Learning has produced some wonderful leaflets about this that you and your child would find helpful and also great fun to use for different writing activities: www.lancsngfl.ac.uk/nationalstrategy/literacy/index.php?category_id=248

Label one A4 sized envelope for each of the six factual text types. Collect a mountain of reading material that can be cut up – newspapers, magazines, leaflets, brochures and perhaps you could even photocopy extracts from books. Sort the text examples into the right envelopes.

Back to basics

You've looked at the physical process of writing, be it with a pen or keyboard. You've looked at the creative side of writing – exciting vocabulary and all the varieties of text, both fact and fiction. There are other things to think about, as you've probably guessed. Not so exciting but definitely necessary. Take a deep breath. Punctuation and spelling. How important are they? Punctuation first.

Punctuation

Read this out loud:

> *one moment she was there on the path the next she was in the forest the black branches closing their arms about her rosy struggled fiercely turning this way and that the more she did the tighter she was held in the embrace of the trees the only escape was forward deeper into the darkness where she had no desire to go but go she must or be strangled the trees had the look of trees that are looked at everything was alive moving the forest had eyes and the eyes were on rosy she glared back not for nothing were her years of training at home defending herself from looks that could kill now she expected nothing else saw nothing else even in eyes that were overflowing with kindness.*

It's not that easy to read because you can't see where to pause or breathe. It isn't split up into paragraphs either. It doesn't make much sense at all. That's the importance of punctuation!

? **A *paragraph* is a collection of sentences all about the same thing.**

Write down sentences and paragraphs with no punctuation and ask your child to add what's missing.

Here are two sentences with the same words, different punctuation:

'Woman, without her man, is nothing.'

'Woman: without her, man is nothing.'

As you can see, the meanings change dramatically.

Does punctuation make you dotty?

Worry no more! Look at Table 4.

Three fun websites

- **Star Punc** contains lots of pieces of text from which the punctuation marks are missing. You have to put the punctuation marks where they belong: www.mape.org.uk/startower/starpunc/index.htm

- **Sparklebox2** has freely downloadable games such as dominoes and bingo – a painless way to learn about punctuation: www.sparklebox2.co.uk/literacy/writing/punct.html

- **BBC Schools Literacy BiteSize Revision** has a great shooting game where you fire punctuation at a sentence, hopefully getting the right symbol in the right place: www.bbc.co.uk/schools/ks2bitesize/english/activities/punctuation.shtml

 Use it or lose it!

Choose a punctuation mark. Together you can say or write a sentence that uses it. Take it in turns using different sorts of punctuation.

Spot the dot

When you're out and about, look out for the punctuation on posters, signs, on the side of buses or in shops. You'll be surprised how often people get it wrong.

Table 4. Common punctuation marks and their main uses

Punctuation mark	Symbol	Uses
Full stop	.	To end a sentence that isn't a question or exclamation: *John ran down the road.*
Question mark	?	To end a sentence that is a question: *How are you? Why do you do that? What's that?*
Exclamation mark	!	To end a sentence that's an exclamation: *Fantastic! Wow! I loved it!*
Comma	,	In a list: *Red, yellow, pink and green.* Before a conjunction: *I hurried, but I was too late.* To show contrast: *The hat was red, not blue, and made of wool.*
Apostrophe	'	To indicate possession: *Dan's coat, children's toys, a dog's tail, dogs' tails* To indicate where letters have been missed out: *Don't (do not), haven't (have not) it's (it is)*
Brackets	( )	To clarify or inform: *My hair was wet (very wet).* For asides and comments: *I didn't do it (honestly!).*
Colon	:	Before a list: *Only four people were present: Jay, Mia, Ali and Jo.* Before a summary: *To summarize: I came, I saw, I conquered.* Before a quote: *As Shakespeare wrote: 'All the world's a stage.'*
Semi-colon	;	To link two sentences that are closely related: *Mum did the washing; there were piles of it.*
Speech marks (sometimes called inverted commas)	'...'	To indicate spoken words: *Meera said, 'Please may I go out tonight?'* *'Go outside at once!' shouted the old man.*
Quotation marks	' ' **or** " "	To indicate quoted words: *'I wandered lonely as a cloud.'*
Hyphen	-	For compound words: *Sister-in-law, X-ray* With prefixes/suffixes: *Pre-meeting, re-evaluate, ex-wife* With numbers: *Thirty-two, two-thirds*
Ellipsis	. . .	When words are left out of a quotation: *'When you walk through a storm . . . don't be afraid of the dark.'* *('hold your head up high and' are the missing words)* To indicate a pause in flow: *Phil laughed and laughed . . . and laughed some more.*

For further details look at: www.correctpunctuation.co.uk/

The most common mistake you'll see is the use of an apostrophe for plurals. For example 'No dog's allowed' or Free-range egg's for sale!' Be proud when you notice!

Spelling

Some people have very strong opinions about spelling. 'If you can understand what someone has written, then it doesn't matter that some of the words are spelled incorrectly.' That would be fine if everyone thought that way. Here are some reasons why correct spelling *is* important, and your support of your child is so important too.

- ■ Creating a bad impression: in the future, when your child takes exams or applies for a job, she is much less likely to be successful if her spelling is poor.

- ■ Being misunderstood: your child might have brilliant ideas, but if no-one can understand her way of spelling then they will be wasted.

- ■ Being anxious: if your child isn't confident about her spelling then she will be unwilling to write at all and particularly to try out new words.

How can you help?

You can help most of all by being encouraging.

As we said before, decide when spelling is on the menu for the day! If the plan is to write an exciting story, don't worry about spellings until later. Now do everything you can to give your child confidence.

You can do this by:

- Looking at words together.
- Talking about spellings.
- Noticing patterns and little words that appear in longer words.
- Encouraging the use of new, exciting words.
- Playing word games.
- Helping with memorizing strategies.
- Concentrating on common mistakes.

Word patterns

Go back to page 30 in the reading section, to refresh your memory about graphemes, digraphs and blends. Now you can definitely see that reading and spelling skills are closely related.

The other patterns that occur in words are *prefixes* and *suffixes*. Knowing the spelling of one of these can help with many words.

A *prefix* is an addition at the beginning of a root word that changes its meaning. Remember the word 'unable' we looked at earlier: /un/ is the prefix that we add to /able/ to make it negative.

A *suffix* is an addition at the end of a root word that changes its meaning. If we add /able/ to the end of the word /manage/ we get 'manageable'.

Knowing the spelling (and the meaning) of lots of prefixes and suffixes makes new words less of a problem.

> **?** A *root word* is a word that has nothing added at the beginning or the end. It stands on its own as a word. It has a meaning. New words can be made from root words by adding beginnings (prefixes) and endings (suffixes) (see Tables 5 and 6).

Table 5. Prefixes

Prefix	+	Root word	=	New word
pre	+	mature	=	premature
sub	+	marine	=	submarine
mis	+	fit	=	misfit
un	+	fortunate	=	unfortunate
extra	+	ordinary	=	extraordinary

Table 6. Suffixes

Root word	+	Suffix	=	New word
dread	+	ful	=	dreadful
knowledge	+	able	=	knowledgeable
high	+	er	=	higher
clever	+	ly	=	cleverly
jump	+	ed	=	jumped

> **Warning** Sometimes, the addition of suffixes changes the spelling of root words. For example, if you add /y/ to /sun/ it becomes 'sunny'.

Word games

Bumper bundles

Perhaps your child has a school project about trees, or wants to write a story about ponies or pirates? Get a big sheet of paper and, together, think of all the words that might be useful. Write them down, concentrating on the spelling. That will make the actual writing much less of a problem.

Wicked words

There are some words that are easy to muddle, such as 'there', 'their' and 'they're', 'affect' and 'effect', 'bought' and 'brought', 'weather' and 'whether', 'to', 'too' and 'two'. Keep a note of these when you come across them. Choose one set then have a sentence race – five sentences using each word correctly.

Crosswords, word searches, hangman and scrabble are other word games you could play.

Memorizing strategies (don't forget these!)

It's impossible to learn every spelling by heart, so the thing to do is come up with some strategies that will help. Some things work for one person but not for another, so take some time with your child deciding which strategy is best for him.

Here's the main one:

Look – Think – Cover – Write – Check

Look at the word carefully. Notice its features – double letters, little words inside bigger words, root words and so on. Talk about them together.

Think about the tricky bits that might cause problems.

Cover the word. Try to see it in your mind.

Write it down (don't look back!).

Check back to see if you're right. If not, think about where you went wrong. Try again.

Have a chant!

Some words lend themselves to chanting the spelling in rhythm. Mississippi (the name of a river) is a well-known example:

'M – I – double S – I – double S – I – double P – I'

It sticks in your brain and you'll never forget it!

Some spelling rules are good to chant too, such as 'I before E except after C'.

Think of tricks

Ne**cess**ary – one collar **(c)** two sleeves **(s)**.

Station**e**ry (meaning writing materials) has an **e** for envelope (as opposed to stationary, meaning standing still).

Medium frequency words

In young children's books there are some words that appear all the time, so it is useful to learn these so-called high frequency words, both to read and to spell. Now your child is older, of course she will come across hundreds of words every day. The list below contains common words that she might expect to see on a regular basis, so they are worth knowing too. Some of them are quite tricky to spell (see p. 64).

⚠️ **Warning** **Please don't use this list to give your child endless dull spelling tests! You could use the words much more creatively.**

above	don't	morning	think
across	during	mother	those
almost	earth	much	thought
along	every	near	through
also	eyes	never	today
always	father	number	together
animal	first	often	told
any	follow(ing)	only	tries
around	found	opened	turn(ed)
asked	friends	other	under
baby	garden	outside	until
balloon	goes	own	upon
before	gone	paper	used
began	great	place	walk(ed)(ing)
being	half	right	watch
below	happy	round	where
better	head	second	while
between	heard	show	white
birthday	high	sister	whole
both	I'm	small	why
brother	important	something	window
brought	inside	sometimes	without
can't	jumped	sound	woke(n)
change	knew	started	word
children	know	still	work
clothes	lady	stopped	world
coming	leave	such	write
didn't	light	suddenly	year
different	might	sure	young
does	money	swimming	

Words, words, everywhere

Choose a word of the day. (That's seven words a week!) Then have it displayed everywhere – on the fridge, on sticky notes on doors and cupboards and mirrors, in the car, on the rabbit hutch and so on.

Or you could:

■ Look them up in a dictionary.

■ Pick three at random and use them in a sentence.

■ Place them into groups according to meaning.

You've looked at speaking and listening, reading and writing, punctuation and spelling.

Now . . . all you have to do is get started!

And remember . . . have fun together! It's the best way to learn.

Useful websites and possible purchases

This is just a selection. It's best to go to a bookshop or online and see material first-hand. You know your child better than anyone.

Children's dictionaries

Oxford University Press: A wonderful range of dictionaries, carefully sorted by age suitability. You can see this at: www.oup.com/oxed/dictionaries/english8to10/

Usborne Books:*The Usborne Illustrated Dictionary* not only contains beautifully illustrated words but also information that will help you and your child further with literacy. You can see this at:
www.usborne.co.uk/catalogue/browse.asp?css=1&subject=L&subcat=LE&id=2366

HarperCollins: *Collins Primary Illustrated Dictionary* is another good, helpful one.

www.harpercollins.co.uk/Content/

Grammar and punctuation

HarperCollins: *Collins Easy Learning Grammar and Punctuation*

Usborne Books: *The Usborne Guide to English Grammar* and *The Usborne Guide to English Punctuation*

Keyboard skills

Dance Mat Typing is a fun site – an introduction to touch typing for children aged 7–11 years. It can be found at www.bbc.co.uk/schools/typing/

Literacy workbooks

DON'T FORGET – you don't need to buy lots of practice books. They can be boring for your child. There are plenty of activities suggested in this book that you can do at home together, using everyday materials, and, what's more, they don't cost anything!

Some workbooks you can buy ARE good fun!

The *Magical Skills* series from Letts are bright and lively, with titles such as *Gruesome Grammar* and *Smelly Spelling.* They are clearly marked with the age range too.

Useful websites

The Primary Framework, which sets out what your child will be taught in school, can be found here: www.standards.dfes.gov.uk/primaryframework/

To help with grammar: www.grammaticallycorrect.co.uk/

To help with punctuation: www.correctpunctuation.co.uk/

To help with factual writing – some fun leaflets: www.lancsngfl.ac.uk/nationalstrategy/literacy/ index.php?category_id=248

To select the most popular children's books: www.richardandjudybookclub.co.uk

Fun literacy websites for your child

The following are only a small selection. There are many out there, especially on the BBC Schools website:

www.bbc.co.uk/schools/ks2bitesize/english/

www.poetry4kids.com

For punctuation:

www.mape.org.uk/startower/starpunc/index.htm

www.sparklebox2.co.uk/literacy/writing/punct.html

www.bbc.co.uk/schools/ks2bitesize/english/activities/punctuation.shtml

To make a puppet theatre:
www.molli.org.uk/burma/theatre/make.htm

More information for you

The National Literacy Trust – ideas and current thinking at www.literacytrust.org.uk

NIACE – for people of all ages who struggle with words (and numbers) in their everyday lives: www.niace.org.uk/

ParentsCentre – lots of information about educational matters and advice for particular needs at www.parentscentre.gov.uk/

The British Dyslexia Association: www.bdadyslexia.org.uk

Being Left-handed – www.lefthandedchildren.org/

www.anythingleft-handed.co.uk/kids_help.html

About ADHD –
www.rcpsych.ac.uk/mentalhealthinformation/mentalhealthandgrowingup/5adhdhyperkineticdisorder.aspx

Appendix 1: Reading and writing levels

Level 3

Pupils read a range of texts fluently and accurately. They read independently, using strategies appropriately to establish meaning. In responding to fiction and non-fiction they show understanding of the main points and express preferences. They use their knowledge of the alphabet to locate books and find information.

Level 4

In responding to a range of texts, pupils show understanding of significant ideas, themes, events and characters, beginning to use inference and deduction. They refer to the text when explaining their views. They locate and use ideas and information.

Level 5

Pupils show understanding of a range of texts, selecting essential points and using inference and deduction where appropriate. In their responses, they identify key features, themes and characters and select sentences, phrases and relevant information to support their views. They retrieve and collate information from a range of sources.

Writing

Level 3

Pupils' writing is often organized, imaginative and clear. The main features of different forms of writing are used appropriately, beginning to be adapted to different readers. Sequences of sentences extend ideas logically and words are chosen for variety and interest. The basic grammatical structure of sentences is usually correct. Spelling is usually accurate, including that of common, polysyllabic words. Punctuation to mark sentences – full stops, capital letters and question marks – is used accurately. Handwriting is joined and legible.

Level 4

Pupils' writing in a range of forms is lively and thoughtful. Ideas are often sustained and developed in interesting ways and organized appropriately for the purpose of the reader. Vocabulary choices are often adventurous and words are used for effect. Pupils are beginning to use grammatically complex sentences, extending meaning. Spelling, including that of polysyllabic words that conform to regular patterns, is generally accurate. Full stops, capital letters and question marks are used correctly, and pupils are beginning to use punctuation within the sentence. Handwriting style is fluent, joined and legible.

Level 5

Pupils' writing is varied and interesting, conveying meaning clearly in a range of forms for different readers, using a more formal style where appropriate. Vocabulary choices are imaginative and words are used precisely.

Simple and complex sentences are organized into paragraphs. Words with complex regular patterns are usually spelled correctly. A range of punctuation, including commas, apostrophes and inverted commas, is usually used accurately. Handwriting is joined, clear and fluent and, where appropriate, is adapted to a range of tasks.

Glossary

Listed below are the specialist terms that are used in this book.

You can download a complete glossary of all the words to do with literacy at www.standards.dfes.gov.uk/primary/publications/literacy/63285/

Acrostic

An *acrostic* is a poetic form which uses the initial letters of a key word.

ADHD

ADHD stands for attention-deficit hyperactivity disorder.

Adjective

An *adjective* is a word that modifies the meaning of a *noun* or *pronoun*, by describing it *(pretty, red)* identifying it *(my, your)* or quantifying it *(many, few, all)*.

Adverb

An *adverb* modifies the meaning of a *verb* and often ends in -ly – *quickly, sadly, unfortunately.*

Alliteration

Alliteration is a series of words that start with the same sound

Analytical phonics

Analytical phonics makes use of each *letter* to build up a word. 'Scan' would be built up from /s/ /c/ /a/ and /n/.

Blending

Blending is to join phonemes (or graphemes) together to make a word, or a bigger chunk of a word. For example, you blend /th/ and /r/ and /ee/ to make the word 'three'.

Closed question

A closed question can be answered with a single word or a short phrase, e.g. What colour is that? How old are you? Are you hot? It can limit speech (see *open question*).

Conjunction

A *conjunction* is a linking word. The most common one is *and*; *but*, *because* and *when* are other examples.

Cursive writing

Cursive writing is joined up writing. *Printing* means writing each letter individually and is much slower.

Dialogue

Dialogue is a conversation that is very much 'give and take' – listening to other points of view, expressing your own, considering alternatives, reaching a common understanding.

Digraph

A digraph is two letters that make up one sound – such as /ch/ and /ph/.

Dyslexia

Dyslexia is a word that comes from Greek meaning 'difficulty with words'.

Formal language

Formal language is most often used between people who don't know each other very well. Complete sentences and precise vocabulary are generally used. Phrases are linked by words such as 'however' and 'therefore' (see *informal language*).

Grapheme

A grapheme is the written letters that represent a sound (a phoneme) It could be a single letter or two or three stuck together. See pages 31–2 for a complete list.

Haiku

A *haiku* is a sort of poem with 17 syllables and three lines; it originated in Japan.

Informal language

Informal language is most often used between friends and family members. Sentences are often incomplete (e.g. 'Sounds great!', 'Could do!') and words are replaced with more casual ones (e.g. Yep or yeah or OK for yes) (see *formal language*).

Kenning

A *kenning* is a bit like a riddle and was used in ancient Norse and Celtic writing. It uses two-word phrases to describe an object.

Limerick

A *limerick* is a five-line poem with a very strict rhyme and form.

Metaphor

A metaphor is like a simile but instead of saying one thing is *like* another, you say it *is* something else. *'You are my sunshine'; 'The world is a stage.'*

Morpheme

The smallest unit of meaning in a word is called a morpheme. A word can contain more than one morpheme. The word *unable* contains the morphemes *able* and *un-* to make it negative. The word *bungalow* is only one morpheme. It cannot be broken down into smaller units of meaning.

Noun

A *noun* is a word used to name a person, animal, place, thing or abstract idea –

Charlie, horse, garden, ironing board and *prayer* are all nouns.

Charlie is a *proper noun* – the name of a specific person, so is written with a capital letter, as is a place name like London.

Onomatopoeia

Onomatopoeia is the use of a word that sounds like its meaning such as *swish* or *smack*.

Open question

An open question invites a longer answer, e.g. 'Why do you think he did that?' 'How are you feeling?' 'What shall we do next?' (see *closed question*).

Paragraph

A paragraph is a collection of sentences all about the same thing.

Phoneme

A phoneme is the name for a single sound. It can be just one letter or a combination, such as /b/ or /igh/. See pages 31–32 for a complete list.

Phonics

Phonics is the study of the link between letters and sounds.

Prefix

A prefix is an addition at the beginning of a root word that changes its meaning. In the word *unable* /un/ is the prefix that we add to /able/ to make it negative.

Preposition

A preposition is a word that generally tells us where something is (*on* the table, *under* the bed, *beside* the gate).

Pronoun

A pronoun is a word used to replace a noun, such as *you, she, they, him, it.*

Root word

A root word is a word that has nothing added at the beginning or the end. It stands on its own as a word. It has a meaning. New words can be made from root words by adding beginnings (prefixes) and endings (suffixes).

Shape (or concrete) poem

A *shape (or concrete) poem* is written in the shape of its subject.

Simile

A simile is a comparison between two different things. *'Her hands were as cold as ice.' 'His hair shone like gold.'*

Suffix

A suffix is an addition at the end of a root word that changes its meaning. If we add /able/ to the end of the word /manage/ we get *manageable*.

Synonym

A synonym is a word that means the same as another, such as *small* and *tiny*.

Syntax

Syntax is the name for the grammatical arrangement of words in sentences.

Synthetic phonics

Synthetic phonics builds up words from its separate *sounds*. 'Scan' in this case, would be built up from the sounds /sc/ and /an/.

Trigraph

Three letters that make up one sound are called trigraphs (such as /igh/).

Verb

A verb is a 'doing' or 'being' word. 'Amir *jumps* over the fence.' 'Ellie *was* in the garden.'

Parenting books that speak for themselves...

'a down-to-earth, pragmatic guide that will leave parents feeling positive and empowered.'

Parents Online

978-0-8264-9159-6

'offers useful starting ideas if you want to contribute to your child's learning.'

Junior, 2006

978-1-8553-9194-9

'Very easy to read and a great introduction into what you can expect your child to be studying and learning.'

My Child magazine, August, 2006

978-0-8264-7379-0

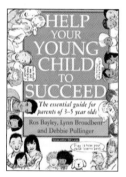

'A marvellous book – informative, accessible, wise. Exactly what busy parents need to ensure the best possible start for their children.'

Sue Palmer, Education consultant and author

978-1-8553-9214-4

New edition of this best-selling book.

'A valuable starting point that won't overwhelm your child.'

Junior, 2006

978-1-8553-9111-6

'I can see how particularly valuable it will be for overactive children in many of our homes.'

From the Foreword by Yehudi Menuhin

978-1-8553-9215-1

continuum

Available now from all good bookshops

www.continuumbooks.com

t: 01202 665432

Parenting books that speak for themselves...

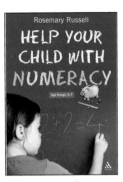

'... offers parents clear descriptions of the ways in which maths is taught in schools today, as well as examples of the kind of calculations children will learn at different ages.'

Jan Winter, Graduate school of Education, University of Bristol

9780826495730

'Refreshingly jargon-free. This book will support parents in having meaningful conversations about maths with their children and so may help make learning numeracy more enjoyable for all.'

Dr Mike Askew, Professor of Mathematics Education, King's College London

9781847064127

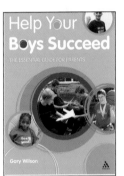

'Really useful and practical. Gives me the full picture and allows me to get involved.'

Quote from a parent

9781855394490

'Highly recommended not only to parents and carers but to all those concerned with the education of the gifted and talented child.'

National Association for the Gifted Child

1855393514

'... offers parents reassurance, encouragement, philosophical perspective and a wealth of practical advice for raising happy, balanced children.'

From the Foreword by Sue Palmer, author of *Toxic Childhood*

9781855394476

'... packed with ideas for encouraging children to start reading and writing, and to want to carry on learning.'

Julia Douëtil, Reading Recovery National Network

9780826495723

continuum

Available now from all good bookshops

www.continuumbooks.com

t: 01202 665432